I0469707

# A Investment
# Platform for Future

# A Investment Platform for Future

## Self Help
## a Self Operating Banking

**Sushanta Kumar Das**

PARTRIDGE
A Penguin Random House Company

**To order additional copies of this book, contact**
Partridge India
000 800 10062 62
orders.india@partridgepublishing.com

www.partridgepublishing.com/india

# CONTENTS

# DEDICATION

This book is a dedication to those peoples
Little earning,
Straggling life long with poor economy,
Dreams for better economy,
They wants few future saving,
Wants a good investment plan,
Economically compromising on every ground for many crisis,
They are choosing cheat funds,
They cheated,
They lost everything by cheat fund .

# PREFACE

To

The Readers


I have to say something about a investment platform. This will give you a extra advantage for your invested many.

A INVESTMENT PLATFORM FOR FUTURE

self help
A self operating bankings

Contains with deposit plans.

| | |
|---|---|
| Subject. | A banking plan for future deposit. |
| Base. | These plans, everyone based on bank's recurring deposit. |
| Formation. | Designed with five different Recurring Deposits. |

A calculation miracle, unbelievable, but is true. These investments will give you almost 63 percent of interest. By these investment, 10 percent banking interest would be increased by 63 percent . Has no duplicacy, has not any fraud, it is following banks term and condition. Could be operated by any person in a bank.

Here has given A to Z details. I am trying to give you every details on these matter,investment graph, maturity value, how would be operating.

This plan will give you mental support.

You will receive a maturity amount each year.

This written is not a calculation accuracy, came from an idea, came from poor economic situation that I had been faced.

Calculation may difference at different bank but fundamental is same.

Savings for future is a common think of ours.

But is not possible for everyone to deposit a big amount at a time.

Otherwise no one that will give you almost 55 percent interest.

It is impossible, but I am trying to get that by change formatically.

Author
SUSHANTA KUMAR DAS

# FEW IMPORTANT CALCULATION

before start

RECURRING DEPOSIT.    Duration 60 months

Instalment 100 per month

|  | Interest 9% |
|---|---|
| 1st year | 1259/- |
| 2nd year | 1259+1372=2631/- |
| 3rd ys. | 1259+2868=4127- |
| 4th ys. | 1259+4498=5757/- |
| 5th ys. | 1259+6275=7534/- |
|  | Interest rate 9.25% |
| 1st ys. | 1260/- |
| 2nd ys. | 1260+1377=2637/- |
| 3rd ys. | 1260+2880=4140/- |
| 4th ys. | 1260+4523=5783/- |
| 5th ys. | 1260+6318=7578- |
|  | Interest rate 9.5% |
| 1st ys. | 1262/- |
| 2nd ys. | 1262+1382=2644/- |
| 3rd ys. | 1262+2895=4157/- |
| 4th ys. | 1262+4552=5814/- |
| 5th ys. | 1262+6366=7628/- |
|  | Interest rate 9.75% |
| 1st ys. | 1263/- |
| 2nd ys. | 1263+1386=2649/- |
| 3rd ys. | 1263+2907=4170/- |
| 4th ys. | 1263+4577=5840/- |
| 5th ys. | 1273+6409=7672/- |
|  | Interest rate-rate 10% |
| 1st ys. | 1265/- |
| 2nd ys. | 1265+1392=2657/- |
| 3rd ys. | 1265+2923=4188/- |
| 4th ys. | 1265+4607=5872/- |
| 5th ys. | 1265+6459=7724/- |

## Monthly instalment 150/-

Interest rate 9%

| | |
|---|---|
| 1st ys. | 1888/- |
| 2nd ys. | 1888+2058=3946/- |
| 3rd ys. | 1888+4301=6189/- |
| 4th ys. | 1888+6746=8634/- |
| 5th ys. | 1888+9411=11299/- |

Interest rate 9.25%

| | |
|---|---|
| 1st ys. | 1890/- |
| 2nd ys. | 1890+2065=3955/- |
| 3rd ys. | 1890+4321=6211/- |
| 4th ys. | 1890+6786=8676- |
| 5th ys. | 1890+9479=11369/- |

Interest rate 9.5%

| | |
|---|---|
| 1st ys. | 1893/- |
| 2nd ys. | 1893+2073=3966/- |
| 3rd ys. | 1893+4343=6236/- |
| 4th ys. | 1893+6828=8721/- |
| 5th ys | 1893 +9549=11442/- |

Interest rate 9.75%

| | |
|---|---|
| 1st ys. | 1895/- |
| 2nd ys. | 1895+2080=3975/- |
| 3rd ys. | 1895+4363=6258/- |
| 4th ys. | 1895+6868=8763/- |
| 5th ys. | 1895+9517=11512/- |

Interest rate 10%

| | |
|---|---|
| 1st ys. | 1898/- |
| 2nd ys. | 1898+2088=3986/- |
| 3rd ys. | 1898+4385=6283/- |
| 4th ys. | 1898+6911=8809/- |
| 5th ys. | 1898+9690=11588/- |

Monthly instalment 200/-

|  | Interest rate 9% |
|---|---|
| 1st ys. | 2517/- |
| 2nd ys. | 2517+2744=5261/- |
| 3rd ys. | 2517+5734=8251/- |
| 4th ys. | 2517+8994=11511/- |
| 5th ys. | 2517+12547=15064/- |
|  | Interest rate 9.25% |
| 1st ys. | 2520/- |
| 2nd ys. | 2520+2753=5273/- |
| 3rd ys. | 2520+5761=8281/- |
| 4th ys. | 2520+9047=11567/- |
| 5th ys. | 2520+12637=15157/- |
|  | Interest rate 9.5% |
| 1st ys. | 2524/- |
| 2nd ys. | 2524+2764=5288/- |
| 3rd ys. | 2524+5761=8281/- |
| 4th ys. | 2524+9047=11567/- |
| 5th ys. | 2524+12733=15257/- |
|  | Interest rate 9.75% |
| 1st ys. | 2527/- |
| 2nd ys. | 2527+2773=5300/- |
| 3rd ys. | 2527+5817=8344/- |
| 4th ys. | 2527+9158=11685/- |
| 5th ys. | 2527+12824=15351/- |
|  | Interest rate 10% |
| 1st ys. | 2530/- |
| 2nd ys. | 2530+2783=5313/- |
| 3rd ys. | 2530+5844=8374/- |
| 4th ys. | 2530+9211=11741/- |
| 5thbys. | 2530+12915=15445/- |

## Monthly instalment 250/-

Interest rate 9%
| | |
|---|---|
| 1st ys. | 3146/- |
| 2nd ys. | 3146+3429=6575/- |
| 3rd ys. | 3146+7167=10313/- |
| 4th ys. | 3146+11241=14387/- |
| 5th ys. | 3146+15682=18828/- |

Interest rate 9.25%
| | |
|---|---|
| 1st ys. | 3150/- |
| 2nd ys. | 3150+3441=6591/- |
| 3rd ys. | 3150+7201=10351/- |
| 4th ys. | 3150+11308=14458/- |
| 5th ys. | 3150+15795=18945/- |

Interest rate 9.5%
| | |
|---|---|
| 1st ys. | 3154/- |
| 2nd ys. | 3154+3454=6608/- |
| 3rd ys. | 3154+7236=10390/- |
| 4th ys. | 3154+11377=14531/- |
| 5th ys. | 3154+15911=19065/- |

Interest rate 9.75%
| | |
|---|---|
| 1st ys. | 3158/- |
| 2nd ys. | 3158+3466=6624/- |
| 3rd ys. | 3158+7270=10428/- |
| 4th ys. | 3158+11445=14603/- |
| 5th ys. | 3158+16027=19185/- |

Interest rate 10%
| | |
|---|---|
| 1st ys. | 3163/- |
| 2nd ys. | 3163+3479=6642/- |
| 3rd ys. | 3163+7306=10469/- |
| 4th ys. | 3163+11516=14679/- |
| 5th ys. | 3163+16147=19310/- |

Monthly investment 300/-

|  | Interest rate 9% |
| --- | --- |
| 1st ys. | 3776/- |
| 2nd ys. | 3776+4116=7892/- |
| 3rd us. | 3776+8602=12378/- |
| 4th ys. | 3776+13492=17268/- |
| 5th ys. | 3777+18822=22598/- |
|  | Interest rate 9.25% |
| 1st ys. | 3780/- |
| 2nd ys. | 3780+4130=7910/- |
| 3rd ys. | 3780+8642=12422/- |
| 4th ys. | 3780+13571=17351/- |
| 5th ys. | 3780+18956=22736/- |
|  | Interest rate 9.5% |
| 1st ys. | 3785/- |
| 2nd ys. | 3785+4145=7930/- |
| 3rd ys. | 3785+8683=12468/- |
| 4th ys. | 3785+13652=17437/- |
| 5th ys. | 3785+19100=22879/- |
|  | Interest rate 9.75% |
| 1st ys. | 3790/- |
| 2nd ys. | 3790+4160=7950/- |
| 3rd ys. | 3790+8725=12515/- |
| 4th ys. | 3790+13735=17525/- |
| 5th ys. | 3790+19234=23024/- |
|  | Interest rate 10% |
| 1st ys. | 3795/- |
| 2nd ys. | 3795+4175=7970/- |
| 3rd ys. | 3795+8767=12562/- |
| 4th ys. | 3795+13818=17613/- |
| 5th ys. | 3795+19374=23169/- |

## Monthly instalment 350/-

Interest rate 9%

| | |
|---|---|
| 1st ys. | 4405/- |
| 2nd ys. | 4405+4801=9206/- |
| 3rd ys. | 4405+10035=14440/- |
| 4th ys. | 4405+15740=20145/- |
| 5th ys. | 4405+21958=26363/- |

Interest rate 9.25%

| | |
|---|---|
| 1st ys. | 4410/- |
| 2nd ys. | 4410+4818=9228/- |
| 3rd ys. | 4410+10082=14492/- |
| 4th ys. | 4410+15833=20243/- |
| 5th ys. | 4410+22115=26525/- |

Interest rate 9.5%

| | |
|---|---|
| 1st ys. | 4416/- |
| 2nd ys. | 4416+4836=9252/- |
| 3rd ys. | 4416+10131=14547/- |
| 4th ys. | 4416+15929=20345/- |
| 5th ys. | 4416+22278=26694/- |

Interest rate 9.75%

| | |
|---|---|
| 1st ys. | 4422/- |
| 2nd ys. | 4422+4853=9275/- |
| 3rd ys. | 4422+10179=14601/- |
| 4th ys. | 4422+16025=20447/- |
| 5th ys. | 4422+22441=26863/- |

Interest rate 10%

| | |
|---|---|
| 1st ys. | 4428/- |
| 2nd ys. | 4428+4871=9299/- |
| 3rd ys. | 4428+10229=14657/- |
| 4th ys. | 4428+16123=20551/- |
| 5th ys. | 4428+22606=27034/- |

Monthly instalment 400/-

Interest rate 9 %

| | |
|---|---|
| 1st ys. | 5034/- |
| 2nd ys. | 5034+5487=10521/- |
| 3rd ys. | 5034+11468=16502/- |
| 4th ys. | 5034+17987=23021/- |
| 5th ys. | 5034+25093=30127/- |

Interest rate 9.25%

| | |
|---|---|
| 1st ys. | 5041/- |
| 2nd ys. | 5041+5507=10548/- |
| 3rd ys. | 5041+11524=16565/- |
| 4th ys. | 5041+18098=23138/- |
| 5th ys. | 5041+25278=30319/- |

Interest rate 9.5%

| | |
|---|---|
| 1st ys. | 5047/- |
| 2nd ys. | 5047+5526=10573/- |
| 3rd us. | 5047+11577=16624/- |
| 4th ys. | 5047+18203=23250/- |
| 5th ys. | 5047+25459=30506/- |

Interest rate 9.75%

| | |
|---|---|
| 1st ys. | 5054/- |
| 2nd ys. | 5054+5547=10601/- |
| 3rd ys. | 5054+11635=16689/- |
| 4th ys. | 5054+18316=23370/- |
| 5th ys. | 5054+25649=30703/- |

Interest rate 10/-

| | |
|---|---|
| 1st ys. | 5060/- |
| 2nd ys. | 5060+5566=10626/- |
| 3rd ys. | 5060+11689=16749/- |
| 4th ys. | 5060+18424=23484/- |
| 5th ys. | 5060+25832=30892/- |

Monthly instalment 450/-

Interest rate 9%
1st ys.       5663/-
2nd ys.      5663+6173=11836/-
3rd ys.      5663+12901=18564/-
4th ys.      5663+20235=25898/-
5th ys.      5663+28229=33892/-

Interest rate 9.25%
1st ys.       5671/-
2nd ys.      5671+6196=11867/-
3rd ys.      5671+12965=18636/-
4th ys.      5671+20360=26031/-
5th ys.      5671+28439=34110/-

Interest rate 9.5%
1st ys.       5678/-
2nd ys.      5678+6217=11895/-
3rd ys.      5678+13025=18703/-
4th ys.      5678+20450=26158/-
5th ys.      5678+28643=34321/-

Interest rate 9.75%
1st ys.       5685/-
2nd ys.      5685+6239=11924/-
3rd ys.      5685+13087=18772/-
4th ys.      5685+20602=26287/-
5th ys.      5685+28850=34535/-

Interest rate 10%
1st ys.       5693/-
2nd ys.      5693+6262=11955/-
3rd ys.      5693+13151=18844/-
4th ys.      5693+20728=26421/-
5th ys.      5693+29063=34756/-

## Monthly instalment 500/-

|          | Interest rate 9%        |
|----------|-------------------------|
| 1st ys.  | 6293/-                  |
| 2nd ys.  | 6293+6859=13152/-       |
| 3rd ys.  | 6293+14336=20629/-      |
| 4th ys.  | 6293+22486=28779/-      |
| 5th ys.  | 6293+31369=37662/-      |

|          | Interest rate 9.25%     |
|----------|-------------------------|
| 1st ys.  | 6301/-                  |
| 2nd ys.  | 6301+6884=13185/-       |
| 3rd ys.  | 6301+14405=20706/-      |
| 4th ys.  | 6301+22621=28922/-      |
| 5th ys.  | 6301+31597=37898/-      |

|          | Interest rate 9.5%      |
|----------|-------------------------|
| 1st ys.  | 6309/-                  |
| 2nd ys.  | 6309+6908=13217/-       |
| 3rd ys.  | 6309+14473=20782/-      |
| 4th ys.  | 6309+22756=29065/-      |
| 5th ys.  | 6309+31826=38135/-      |

|          | Interest rate 9.75%     |
|----------|-------------------------|
| 1st ys.  | 6317/-                  |
| 2nd ys.  | 6317+6933=13250/-       |
| 3rd ys.  | 6317+14542=20859/-      |
| 4th ys.  | 6317+22893=29210/-      |
| 5th ys.  | 6317+32058=38375/-      |

|          | Interest rate 10%       |
|----------|-------------------------|
| 1st ys.  | 6325/-                  |
| 2nd ys.  | 6325+6958=13283/-       |
| 3rd ys.  | 6325+14611=20936/-      |
| 4th ys.  | 6325+23030=29355/-      |
| 5th ys.  | 6325+32291=38616/-      |

# FIXT DEPOSIT

### Investment 100/-    Duration period 15years.

Years.   Interest rate 9%

| 1. | 2. | 3. | 4. | 5. | 6. | 7. | 8 |
|----|----|----|----|----|----|----|----|
| 109. | 119. | 130. | 141. | 154. | 168. | 183. | 199 |

| 9. | 10. | 11. | 12. | 13. | 14. | 15 |
|----|-----|-----|-----|-----|-----|-----|
| 217 | 237. | 258. | 281. | 307 | 334. | 364 |

Years.   Interest rate 9.25%

| 1. | 2. | 3. | 4. | 5. | 6. | 7. | 8 |
|----|----|----|----|----|----|----|----|
| 109. | 119. | 130. | 142. | 156 | 170. | 186. | 203 |

| 9. | 10. | 11 | 12. | 13. | 14. | 15 |
|----|-----|----|-----|-----|-----|-----|
| 222. | 242. | 265. | 289 | 316. | 345 | 377 |

Years.   Interest rate 9.5%

| 1. | 2. | 3. | 4. | 5. | 6. | 7. | 8 |
|----|----|----|----|----|----|----|----|
| 110 | 120 | 131. | 144 | 157 | 172 | 189. | 207 |

| 9. | 10. | 11. | 12. | 13. | 14. | 15 |
|----|-----|-----|-----|-----|-----|-----|
| 226. | 248. | 271. | 297. | 325. | 356. | 390 |

Years.   Interest rate 9.75%

| 1. | 2. | 3. | 4. | 5. | 6. | 7. | 8 |
|----|----|----|----|----|----|----|----|
| 110. | 120. | 132. | 145. | 159. | 175. | 192. | 210 |

| 9. | 10. | 11. | 12. | 13 | 14 | 15 |
|----|-----|-----|-----|----|----|-----|
| 231. | 254. | 278. | 305. | 335. | 368 | 404 |

Years.   Interest rate 10%

| 1. | 2. | 3. | 4. | 5. | 6. | 7. | 8 |
|----|----|----|----|----|----|----|----|
| 110. | 121. | 133. | 146. | 161. | 177. | 195. | 214 |

| 9. | 10. | 11. | 12. | 13. | 14. | 15 |
|----|-----|-----|-----|-----|-----|-----|
| 236. | 259. | 285. | 314. | 345. | 380. | 418 |

# ALTERNATIVE RECURRING DEPOSIT PLAN

calculation on Instalment 100 per month for each RD

  Interest rate   10%
  Bace.           Recurring deposit
  Formation.      Designed with number of 5 recurring deposits.

## A. GRAPH TABLE

Graph of base form of alternative recurring deposit

1st graph

| | |
|---|---|
| 1st year | Opening |
| 2nd year. | Opening |
| 3rd year. | Opening |
| 4th year. | Opening |
| 5th year. | Maturity. Opening |
| 6th year | Maturity. Opening |
| 7th year. | Maturity. Opening |
| 8th year. | Maturity. Opening |
| 9th year. | Maturity. Opening |
| 10th year. | Maturity. Opening |
| 11th year. | Maturity. Opening |
| 12th year. | Maturity. Opening |
| 13th year. | Maturity. Opening |
| 14th year. | Maturity Opening |
| 15th year. | Maturity. Opening |
| 16th year. | Maturity Opening |
| 17th year. | Maturity Opening |
| 18th year. | Maturity Opening |
| 19th year. | Maturity Opening |
| 20th year. | Maturity Opening |

You will receive an amount of maturity many every year.

## 2nd graph

| | | | |
|---|---|---|---|
| After 1st year. | 1opening | | |
| 2nd year. | 1opening. | 1opened | |
| 3. | 1opening. | 2opened | |
| 4. | 1opening. | 3opened | |
| 5. | 1opening. | 4opened | |
| 6. | 1maturity. | 1opening. | 4opened |
| 7. | 1maturity. | 1opening. | 4opened |
| 8. | 1maturity. | 1opening. | 4opened |
| 9. | 1maturity. | 1opening. | 4opened |
| 10. | 1maturitu. | 1opening. | 4opened |
| 11. | 1maturity. | 1opening. | 4opened |
| 12. | 1maturity. | 1opening. | 4opened |
| 13. | 1maturity. | 1opening. | 4opened |
| 14. | 1maturity. | 1opening | 4opened |
| 15. | 1maturity | 1opening. | 4opened |
| 16. | 1maturity. | 4opened | |
| 17. | 1maturity. | 3opened | |
| 18. | 1maturity. | 2opened | |
| 19. | 1maturity. | 1opened | |
| 20. | 1maturity | | |

## B. INVESTMENT TABLE

Investment/Number of RD/Duration (months)
=Total Investment

| | | |
|---|---|---|
| 1st year. | $100 \times 1 \times 12 = 1200$ |
| 2nd year | $100 \times 2 \times 12 = 2400$ |
| 3rd year. | $100 \times 3 \times 12 = 3600$ |
| 4th year. | $100 \times 4 \times 12 = 4800$ |
| 5th year. | $100 \times 5 \times 12 = 6000$ |
| 6th year. | $100 \times 5 \times 12 = 6000$ |
| 7th year. | $100 \times 5 \times 12 = 6000$ |
| 8th year. | $100 \times 5 \times 12 = 6000$ |
| 9th year. | $100 \times 5 \times 12 = 6000$ |
| 10th year. | $100 \times 5 \times 12 = 6000$ |
| 11th year. | $100 \times 5 \times 12 = 6000$ |
| 12th year. | $100 \times 5 \times 12 = 6000$ |
| 13th year. | $100 \times 5 \times 12 = 6000$ |
| 14th year. | $100 \times 5 \times 12 = 6000$ |
| 15th year. | $100 \times 5 \times 12 = 6000$ |
| 16th year. | $100 \times 5 \times 12 = 6000$ |
| 17th year. | $100 \times 5 \times 12 = 6000$ |
| 18th year. | $100 \times 5 \times 12 = 6000$ |
| 19th year. | $100 \times 5 \times 12 = 6000$ |
| 20th year. | $100 \times 5 \times 12 = 6000$ |

You have to invest 6000 per year .

## C. MATURITY TABLE

| Duration (months). | | Yearly Investment. | Maturity |
|---|---|---|---|
| After 1st year. | 12 | 1200. | 0 |
| 2nd. | 12. | 2400. | 0 |
| 3rd. | 12. | 3600. | 0 |
| 4. | 12. | 4800. | 0 |
| 5. | 12. | 6000 | 7724 |
| 6. | 12. | 6000. | 7724 |
| 7. | 12. | 6000. | 7724 |
| 8. | 12. | 6000. | 7724 |
| 9. | 12. | 6000. | 7724 |
| 10. | 12. | 6000. | 7724 |
| 11. | 12. | 6000. | 7724 |
| 12. | 12. | 6000. | 7724 |
| 13. | 12. | 6000. | 7724 |
| 14. | 12. | 6000. | 7724 |
| 15. | 12. | 6000. | 7724 |
| 16. | 12. | 6000. | 7724 |
| 17. | 12. | 6000. | 7724 |
| 18. | 12. | 6000. | 7724 |
| 19. | 12. | 6000. | 7724 |
| 20. | 12. | 6000. | 7724 |

You will receive maturity value 7724 every year .

## D. RECEIVING INTEREST TABLE

| Investment per year. | | Maturity per year. | Interest per year |
|---|---|---|---|
| After 1st year. | 1200. | 0. | 0 |
| 2nd. | 2400. | 0. | 0 |
| 3. | 3600. | 0. | 0 |
| 4. | 4800. | 0. | 0 |
| 5. | 6000. | 7724. | 1724 |
| 6. | 6000. | 7724. | 1724 |
| 7. | 6000. | 7724. | 1724 |
| 8. | 6000. | 7724. | 1724 |
| 9. | 6000. | 7724. | 1724 |
| 10. | 6000. | 7724. | 1724 |
| 11. | 6000. | 7724. | 1724 |
| 12. | 6000. | 7724. | 1724 |
| 13. | 6000. | 7724. | 1724 |
| 14. | 6000. | 7724. | 1724 |
| 15. | 6000. | 7724. | 1724 |
| 16. | 6000. | 7724. | 1724 |
| 17. | 6000. | 7724. | 1724 |
| 18. | 6000. | 7724. | 1724 |
| 19. | 6000. | 7724. | 1724 |
| 20. | 6000. | 7724. | 1724 |

You will receive interest 1724 every year.

## E. COMPLETE DETAILS TABLE

| Monthly investment. | | Number of Rd. | Duration (months). | Total investment. | Maturity. | Interest |
|---|---|---|---|---|---|---|
| After 1st year. | 100 | 1 | 12 | 1200 | 0 | 0 |
| 2nd. | 100 | 2 | 12 | 2400 | 0 | 0 |
| 3. | 100 | 3 | 12 | 3600 | 0 | 0 |
| 4. | 100 | 4 | 12 | 4800 | 0 | 0 |
| 5. | 100 | 5 | 12 | 6000 | 7724 | 1724 |
| 6. | 100 | 5 | 12 | 6000 | 7724 | 1724 |
| 7. | 100 | 5 | 12 | 6000 | 7724 | 1724 |
| 8. | 100 | 5 | 12 | 6000 | 7724 | 1724 |
| 9. | 100 | 5 | 12 | 6000 | 7724 | 1724 |
| 10. | 100 | 5 | 12 | 6000 | 7724 | 1724 |
| 11. | 100 | 5 | 12 | 6000 | 7724 | 1724 |
| 12. | 100 | 5 | 12 | 6000 | 7724 | 1724 |
| 13. | 100 | 5 | 12 | 6000 | 7724 | 1724 |
| 14. | 100 | 5 | 12 | 6000 | 7724 | 1724 |
| 15. | 100 | 5 | 12 | 6000 | 7724 | 1724 |
| 16. | 100 | 5 | 12 | 6000 | 7724 | 1724 |
| 17. | 100 | 5 | 12 | 6000 | 7724 | 1724 |
| 18. | 100 | 5 | 12 | 6000 | 7724 | 1724 |
| 19. | 100 | 5 | 12 | 6000 | 7724 | 1724 |
| 20. | 100 | 5 | 12 | 6000 | 7724 | 1724 |

# HOW TO DO?

## ALTERNATIVE RECURRING DEPOSIT

It could be operated in a bank.

So, first you have to choose a bank, mostly preferred, mostly trusted, mostly liable as your choise that you are thinking, could be depended on it.

And then you have to open a recurring deposit at every year with same investment and with same priod

Monthly instalment 100 or 2,3,4,5 multiple.

Priod- 5years or 60 months.

This investment plan will start after 4 years and after 5 years you will receive a same maturity amount at every year, that may be 1,2, or 100years.

I thing you have not need that you understand it's mathematics.

Just you open a recurring deposit at every year and it would be following automatically.

You will receive same amount of maturity many every year.

You will get an amount of many every year that means would be good mental support.

1st year

You open a RD

2nd year

You open a another RD        1 opened

You have now 2 RD to deposit.

3rd year

You open another one RD        2 opened

You have now 3 RD to deposit.

4th year

You open a RD at 4th year.        3opened

You have now 4RD to deposit.

5th year

Finally on 5th year you open a RD.        4 opened

Now you have to deposit for 5 RD.

6th year

You will receive a maturity.

You have 4 previous RD and you open a RD at this year.

Finally you have to deposit for 5 RD.

After 5th year you will receive same benefit at every year.

And After years You will receive a maturity and you have to open a new one.

On running you have to deposit 5×12×100 =6000/- and you will be receiving 7724/-.

Geometrically Parallelogram shape will give you a maturity many every

Year and you have to open a new one.

This plan will give you almost 53% of interest.

# Comparing
# ALTERNATIVE RECURRING WITH RECURRING
# DEPOSIT

Investment table

ALTERNATIVE RECURRING DEPOSIT
Yeatly
1200×5×1year=6000/-

RECURRING DEPOSIT
Yearly
6000×1×1year=6000/-

maturity table

ALTERNATIVE RECURRING DEPOSIT
Yearly
6000/-          7724/-

RECURRING DEPOSIT
Yeary
6000/-          6325/-

Interest table

ALTERNATIVE RECURRING DEPOSITS

Interest rate (500×?×6.5years)÷100= 1724
$$1724×100$$
$$?=(1724×100)÷(500×6.5)$$
$$?=53\%$$

# RECURRING DEPOSIT

Interest rate- 10%

## COMPLETE DETAILS TABLE

Alternative recurring deposits

| Deposit. | Maturity. | Interest |
|----------|-----------|----------|
| 6000/- | 7724/- | 1724/- |

Recurring deposits

| Deposit. | Maturity | Interest |
|----------|----------|----------|
| 6000/- | 6325/- | 325/- |

# FEW EXAMPLE CALCULATIONS
# ON
# ALTERNATIVE RECURRING DEPOSITS

Monthly Investment 100/-

Interest rate 9% per year
Monthly invest×number of RD×duration
=total deposit--matudity--interest


| 1st y. | 100×1×12 |
| 2nd ys. | 100×2×12 |
| 3rd ys. | 100×3×12 |
| 4th ys. | 100×4×12 |
| 5th ys. | 100×5×12=6000--7534--1534 |


Interest rate- 9.25%/year
100×5×12=6000-7578-1578


Interest rate- 9.5%/year
100×5×12=6000-7628-1628


Interest rate- 9.75%/year
100×5×12=6000-7672-1672


Interest rate- 10%/year
100×5×12=6000-7724-1724

Monthly investment- 150/-

M,ly investment/ number of RD/duration
=total invest-maturity-interest

After
Interest rate- 9%/year
1st year.        150×1×12
2nd year.       150×2×12
3rd.            150×3×12
4th.            150×4×12
5th.            150×5×12=9000-11299-2299

Interest rate-9.25%/year
150×5×12=9000-11369-2369

Interest rate- 9.5%/year
150×5×12=9000-11442-2442

Interest rate- 9.75%/year
150×5×12=9000-11512-2512

Interest rate- 10%/year
150×5×12=9000-11588-2588

Monthly investment- 200/-

Monthly invest/number of RD/duration=total
invest-maturity-interest


Interest rate-9%/year
After
1st year.       200×1×12
2nd.            200×2×12
3rd.            200×3×12
4th.            200×4×12
5th.            200×5×12=12000-15064-3064


Interest rate- 9.25%/year
200×5×12=12000-15157-3157


Interest rate- 9.5%/year
200×5×12=12000-15257-3257


Interest rate- 9.75%/year
200×5×12=12000-15351-3351


Interest rate - 10%/year
200×5×12=12000-15445-3445

Monthly investment- 250/-

Monthly invest/number of RD/duration
=total invest a maturity a interest

Interest rate- 9%
After
1st year.      250×1×12
2nd.          250×2×12
3rd.          250×3×12
4th.          250×4×12
5th.          250×5×12=15000-18828-3828

Interest rate- 9.25%/year
250×5×12=15000-18945-3945

Interest rate- 9.5%/year
250×5×12=15000-19065-4065

Interest rate- 9.75%/year
250×5×12=15000-19185-4185

Interest rate- 10%/year
250×5×12=15000-19310-4310

Monthly investment- 300/-

Monthly invest/number of RD/duration
=total-maturity-interest

After
Interest rate- 9%/year
1st year.        300×1×12
2nd.             300×2×12
3rd.             300×3×12
4th.             300×4×12
5th.             300×5×12=18000-22598-4598

Interest rate- 9.25%/year
300×5×12=18000-22736-4736

Interest rate- 9.5%/year
300×5×12=18000-22879-4879

Interest rate- 9.75%/year
300×5×12=18000-23024-5024

Interest rate- 10%/year
300×5×12=18000-23169-5169

Monthly investment- 350/-

Monthly invest/number of RD/duration
=total invest-maturity-interest

Interest rate- 9%/year
After
1st year        350×1×12
2nd.            350×2×12
3rd.            350×3×12
4th.            350×4×12
5th.            350×5×12=21000-26363-5363

Interest rate- 9.25%/year
350×5×12=21000-26525-5525

Interest rate- 9.5%/year
350×5×12=21000-26694-5694

Interest rate- 9.75%/year
350×5×12=21000-26863-5863

Interest rate- 10%/year
350×5×12=21000-27034-6034

Monthly investment- 400/-

Monthly invest/number of RD/duration
=total invest-maturity-interest


Interest rate- 9%/year
After
1st year.        400×1×12
2nd.             400×2×12
3rd.             400×3×12
4th.             400×4×12
5th.             400×5×12=24000-30127-6127


Interest rate- 9.25%/year
400×5×12=24000-30319-6319


Interest rate- 9.5%/year
400×5×12=24000-30506-6506


Interest rate- 9.75%/year
400×5×12=24000-30703-6703


Interest rate- 10%/year
400×5×12=24000-30892-6892

Monthly investment- 450/-

Monthly invest/number of RD/duration
=total invest a maturity a interest

Interest rate- 9%/year
After
1st year.          450×1×12
2nd.               450×2×12
3rd.               450×3×12
4th.               450×4×12
5th.               450×5×12=27000-33892-6892

Interest rate- 9.25%/year
450×5×12=27000-34110-7110

Interest rate- 9.5%/year
450×5×12=27000-34321-7321

Interest rate- 9.75%/year
450×5×12=27000-34535-7535

Interest rate- 10%/year
450×5×12=27000-34756-7756

Monthly investment- 500/-

Monthly invest/number of RD/duration
=total invest a maturity a interest

Interest rate- 9%/year
After
1st year.        500×1×12
2nd.             500×2×12
3rd.             500×3×12
4th.             500×4×12
5th.             500×5×12=30000-37662-7662

Interest rate- 9.25%/year
500×5×12=30000-37898-7898

Interest rate- 9.5%/year
500×5×12=30000-38135-8135

Interest rate- 9.75%/year
500×5×12=30000-38375-8375

Interest rate- 10%/year
500×5×12=30000-38616-8616

# ALTERNATIVE FIXT DEPOSIT

Monthly instalment 100/-
Number of RD 5
Interest rate 10%
Duration of each RD 5 years

## A. GRAPH TABLE

First graph

| After | | |
|---|---|---|
| 1st year. | | Opening |
| 2nd. | | Opening |
| 3rd. | | Opening |
| 4th. | | Opening |
| 5th. | | Opening |
| 6th. | Maturity. | Opening |
| 7th. | Maturity. | Opening |
| 8th. | Maturity. | Opening |
| 9th. | Maturity. | Opening |
| 10th. | Maturity. | Opening |
| 11th. | Maturity. | Opening |
| 12th. | Maturity. | Opening |
| 13th. | Maturity. | Opening |
| 14th. | Maturity. | Opening |
| 15th. | Maturity. | Opening |
| 16th. | Maturity. | |
| 17th. | Maturity. | |
| 18th. | Maturity. | |
| 19th. | Maturity. | |
| 20th. | Maturity | |

## Second graph

| | | |
|---|---|---|
| 1st year. | 0 | |
| 2nd. | 0 | |
| 3rd. | 0 | |
| 4th. | 0 | |
| 5th. | 0 | |
| 6th | 7724. | 15years |
| 7th. | 7724. | 14yrars |
| 8th. | 7724. | 13ys. |
| 9th. | 7724. | 12ys. |
| 10th. | 7724. | 11ys. |
| 11th. | 7724. | 10ys. |
| 12th. | 7724. | 09ys. |
| 13th. | 7724. | 08ys. |
| 14th. | 7724. | 07ys. |
| 15th. | 7724. | 06ys. |
| 16th. | 7724. | 05ys. |
| 17th. | 7724. | 04ys. |
| 18th. | 7724. | 03ys. |
| 19th. | 7724. | 02ys. |
| 20th. | 7724. | 01y. |

After 20th year = total maturity

## B. INVESTMENT TABLE

### Investment Table1

Monthly invest×Number of RD×Dration(months)
= Total invest

After

| | |
|---|---|
| 1st year. | 100×1×12=1200 |
| 2nd. | 100×2×12=2400 |
| 3rd. | 100×3×12=3600 |
| 4th. | 100×4×12=4800 |
| 5th. | 100×5×12=6000 |
| 6th. | 100×5×12=6000 |
| 7th. | 100×5×12=6000 |
| 8th. | 100×5×12=6000 |
| 9th. | 100×5×12=6000 |
| 10th. | 100×5×12=6000 |
| 11th. | 100×5×12=6000 |
| 12th. | 100×5×12=6000 |
| 13th. | 100×5×12=6000 |
| 14th. | 100×5×12=6000 |
| 15th. | 100×5×12=6000 |
| 16th. | 100×4×12=4800 |
| 17th. | 100×3×12=3600 |
| 18th. | 100×2×12=2400 |
| 19th. | 100×1×12=1200 |

## Investment Table 2

After

| | |
|---|---|
| 1st year. | 0 |
| 2nd. | 0 |
| 3rd. | 0 |
| 4th. | 0 |
| | (received maturity value from altrlernative RD) |
| 5th. | 6000+1724 for 15years |
| 6th. | 6000+1724 for 14ys. |
| 7th. | 6000+1724 for 13ys. |
| 8th. | 6000+1724 for 12ys. |
| 9th. | 6000+1724 for 11ys. |
| 10th. | 6000+1724 for 10ys. |
| 11th. | 6000+1724 for 09ys. |
| 12th. | 6000+1724 for 08ys. |
| 13th. | 6000+1724 for 07ys. |
| 14th. | 6000+1724 for 06ys. |
| 15th. | 6000+1724 for 05ys. |
| 16th. | 6000+1724 for 04ys. |
| 17th. | 6000+1724 for 03ys. |
| 18th. | 6000+1724 for 02ys. |
| 19th. | 6000+1724 for 01year. |

Total investment= 90000

## C. MATURITY TABLE

### Maturity Table 1

| After | Investment | Maturity value |
|---|---|---|
| 1st. Year | 1200 | |
| 2nd. | 2400 | |
| 3rd. | 3600 | |
| 4th. | 4800 | |
| 5th. | 6000. | 7724 |
| 6th. | 6000. | 7724 |
| 7th. | 6000. | 7724 |
| 8th. | 6000. | 7724 |
| 9th. | 6000. | 7724 |
| 10th. | 6000. | 7724 |
| 11th. | 6000. | 7724 |
| 12th. | 6000. | 7724 |
| 13th. | 6000. | 7724 |
| 14th. | 6000. | 7724 |
| 15th. | 6000. | 7724 |
| 16th. | 4800. | 7724 |
| 17th. | 3600. | 7724 |
| 18th. | 2400. | 7724 |
| 19th. | 1200. | 7724 |
| 20th. | 0. | 7724 |

| Total =Invest. | Maturity value |
|---|---|
| 90000/- | 115810/- |

maturity table 2

| | Investment. | Maturity Value |
|---|---|---|
| 1st invest. | 00000 | |
| 2nd invest. | 00000 | |
| 3rd invest. | 00000 | |
| 4th invest. | 00000 | |
| 5th invest. | 00000 | |
| 6th invest. | 7724. | 32265 |
| 7th invest. | 7724. | 29332 |
| 8th invest. | 7724. | 26665 |
| 9th invest. | 7724. | 24241 |
| 10th invest. | 7724. | 22037 |
| 11th invest. | 7724. | 20034 |
| 12th invest. | 7724. | 18213 |
| 13th invest. | 7722. | 16557 |
| 14th invest. | 7724. | 15052 |
| 15th invest. | 7724. | 13684 |
| 16th invest. | 7724. | 12440 |
| 17th invest. | 7724. | 11309 |
| 18th invest. | 7724. | 10281 |
| 19th invest. | 7724. | 9346 |
| 20th invest. | 7724. | 8496 |

Total investment 90000/-
Total maturity 269916/-

## D. INTEREST TABLE

Invest/Received Interest after each year/received Interest finally

After

| | |
|---|---|
| 1st year. | 0 |
| 2nd year. | 0 |
| 3rd year. | 0 |
| 4th year. | 0 |
| 5th year. | 6000/1724/26265 |
| 6th year. | 6000/1724/23332 |
| 7th year. | 6000/1724/20665 |
| 8th year. | 6000/1724/18241 |
| 9th year. | 6000/1724/16037 |
| 10th year. | 6000/1724/14034 |
| 11th year. | 6000/1724/12213 |
| 12th year. | 6000/1724/10557 |
| 13th year. | 6000/1724/9052 |
| 14th year. | 6000/1724/7684 |
| 15th year. | 6000/1724/6440 |
| 16th year. | 4800/2924/5309 |
| 17th year. | 3600/4124/4281 |
| 18th year. | 2400/5324/3346 |
| 19th year. | 1200/6724/2496 |

Total Received Interest- 179916/-

# HOW TO DO?

## Alternative fixt deposit.

How to do?
Could be operating in a bank as others.
You have need to select a your preffered bank.
First follow to ALTERNATIVE RECURRING DEPOSIT,
You will receive a same amount of many every year.
And then you have need to deposit it.
Each year's received many deposit it to mature at a same date.

|       | Investment date(received many each year). | Maturity date |
|-------|------------------------------------|----------------|
| 1st.  | No                                 |                |
| 2nd.  | No                                 |                |
| 3rd.  | No                                 |                |
| 4th.  | No                                 |                |
| 5th.  | No                                 |                |
| 6th.  | 01st Jan,2006.                     | 01st Jan,2021  |
| 7th.  | 01st Jan,2007.                     | 01st Jan,2021  |
| 8th.  | 01/01/2008----------01/01/2021     |                |
| 9th.  | 01/01/2009----------01/01/2021     |                |
| 10th. | 01/01/2010----------01/01/2021     |                |
| 11th. | 01/01/2011----------01/01/2021     |                |
| 12th. | 01/01/2012----------01/01/2021     |                |
| 13th. | 01/01/2013----------01/01/2021     |                |
| 14th. | 01/01/2014----------01/01/2021     |                |
| 15th. | 01/01/2015----------01/01/2021     |                |

16th.  01/01/2016----------01/01/2021
17th.  01/01/2017----------01/01/2021
18th.  01st Jan,2018.      01st Jan,2021
19th.  01st Jan,2019.      01st Jan,2021
20th.  01st Jan,2020.      01st Jan,2021

Final maturitu on 01st Jan,2021

Graph 1 will give you almost 53% and graph 2 will give you 10% of interest. Totally almost 63% you will get.

# COMPARE WITH FIXT DEPOSIT

Investment table

Recurring fixt deposit
Deposif amount.          90000/-

Fist deposit
Deposit amount.          90000/-

Maturity table

Recurring fixt deposit
Matirity amount.          269916/-

Fixt deposit
Maturity amount.          209699/-

Interest table

Recurring fixt deposit
Received interest amount.          179916/-

Fixt deposit
Received interest amount.          119699/-

Otherwise for fixt deposit, you have need a amount at a time.
I used here recurring deposit to this porpose.
So, you have no need a amount at a time.

# FEW EXAMPLE CALCULATION

RD Instalment. 100 per month

| After | 9% | 9.25% | 9.5% | 9.75% | 10% |
|---|---|---|---|---|---|
| 6th year. | 8212. | 8279. | 8353. | 8420. | 8496 |
| 7th year. | 8951. | 9045. | 9146. | 9241. | 9346 |
| 8th year. | 9756. | 9881. | 10015. | 10142. | 10281 |
| 9th year. | 10635. | 10795. | 10966. | 11131. | 11309 |
| 10th year. | 11592. | 11794. | 12008. | 12216. | 12440 |
| 11th year. | 12635. | 12885. | 13149. | 13407. | 13684 |
| 12th year. | 13772. | 14077. | 14398. | 14714. | 15052 |
| 13th year. | 15012. | 15379. | 15766. | 16149. | 16557 |
| 14th year. | 16363. | 16801. | 17264. | 17723. | 18213 |
| 15th year. | 17836. | 18356. | 18904. | 19452. | 20034 |
| 16th year. | 19441. | 20054. | 20700. | 21348. | 22037 |
| 17th year. | 21191. | 21908. | 22666. | 23423. | 24241 |
| 18th year. | 23098. | 23935. | 24820. | 25714. | 26665 |
| 19th year. | 25177. | 26149. | 27177. | 28221. | 29332 |
| 20th year. | 27442. | 28568. | 29759. | 30973. | 32265 |

| Total Maturity. | 241113. | 247906. | 255091. | 262280. | 269916 |

## RD Instalment - 150/month

| After | 9% | 9.25% | 9.5% | 9.75% | 10% |
|---|---|---|---|---|---|
| 6th year. | 12316. | 12421. | 12529. | 13634. | 12747 |
| 7th year. | 13424. | 13570. | 13719. | 13866. | 14021 |
| 8th year. | 14632. | 14825. | 15023. | 15218. | 15424 |
| 9th year. | 15949. | 16196. | 16450. | 16702. | 16966 |
| 10th year. | 17384. | 17694. | 18012. | 18330. | 18663 |
| 11th year. | 18949. | 19331. | 19724. | 20118. | 20529 |
| 12th year. | 20654. | 21119. | 21597. | 22079. | 22582 |
| 13th year. | 22513. | 23072. | 23649. | 24232. | 24840 |
| 14th year. | 24540. | 25207. | 25896. | 26594. | 27324 |
| 15th year. | 26748. | 27538. | 28356. | 29187. | 30056 |
| 16th year. | 29155. | 30086. | 31050. | 32033. | 33062 |
| 17th year. | 31779. | 32868. | 33999. | 35156. | 36368 |
| 18th year. | 34640. | 35909. | 37229. | 38584. | 40005 |
| 19th year. | 37757. | 39230. | 40766. | 42346. | 44005 |
| 20th year. | 41155. | 42859. | 44639. | 46475. | 48406 |
| | | | | | |
| Total Maturity. | 361595. | 371925. | 382638. | 393554. | 404998 |

## RD Instalment - 200/month

| After | 9% | 9.25% | 9.5% | 9.75% | 10% |
|---|---|---|---|---|---|
| 6th year. | 16420. | 16559. | 16705. | 16848. | 16990 |
| 7th year. | 17898. | 18091. | 18294. | 18490. | 18688 |
| 8th year. | 19508. | 19764. | 20031. | 20293. | 20557 |
| 9th year. | 21264. | 21592. | 21934. | 22272. | 22613 |
| 10th year. | 23178. | 23590. | 24012. | 24443. | 24874 |
| 11th year. | 25264. | 25772. | 26300. | 26826. | 27362 |
| 12th year. | 27538. | 28156. | 28798. | 29442. | 30098 |
| 13th year. | 30016. | 30760. | 31534. | 32313. | 33108 |
| 14th year. | 32717. | 33605. | 34530. | 35463. | 36419 |
| 15th year. | 35662. | 36714. | 37810. | 38921. | 40060 |
| 16th year. | 38872. | 40110. | 41402. | 42716. | 44066 |
| 17th year. | 42370. | 43820. | 45336. | 46880. | 48473 |
| 18th year. | 46183. | 47843. | 49642. | 51451. | 53320 |
| 19th year. | 50340. | 52301. | 54358. | 56468. | 58652 |
| 20th year. | 54870. | 57139. | 59522. | 61973. | 64518 |

| Total Maturity. | 482095. | 495846. | 510214. | 524799. | 539798 |

## RD Instalment - 250/month

| After | 9% | 9.25% | 9.5% | 9.75% | 10% |
|---|---|---|---|---|---|
| 6th year. | 19869. | 20697. | 20875. | 21056. | 21241 |
| 7th year. | 21657. | 22612. | 22859. | 23108. | 23365 |
| 8th year. | 23715. | 24704. | 25031. | 25362. | 25702 |
| 9th year. | 25848. | 27050. | 27409. | 27834. | 28272 |
| 10th year. | 28175. | 29552. | 30013. | 30548. | 31099 |
| 11th year. | 30710. | 32286. | 32864. | 33527. | 34209 |
| 12th year. | 33474. | 35273. | 35986. | 36795. | 37630 |
| 13th year. | 36487. | 38535. | 39405. | 40383. | 41393 |
| 14th year. | 39770. | 42100. | 43148. | 44320. | 45532 |
| 15th year. | 43350. | 45994. | 47247. | 48642. | 50085 |
| 16th year. | 47251. | 50248. | 51736. | 53384. | 55094 |
| 17th year. | 51504. | 54896. | 56651. | 58589. | 60603 |
| 18th year. | 56139. | 59974. | 62033. | 64301. | 66663 |
| 19th year. | 61191. | 65522. | 67926. | 70571. | 73330 |
| 20th year. | 66700. | 71583. | 74379. | 77451. | 80663 |
| Total Maturity. | 585841. | 621026. | 637562. | 655871. | 674881 |

## RD Instalment - 300/month

| After | 9% | 9.25% | 9.5% | 9.75% | 10% |
|---|---|---|---|---|---|
| 6th year. | 24632. | 24839. | 25053. | 25269. | 25486 |
| 7th year. | 26849. | 27137. | 27432. | 27733. | 28034 |
| 8th year. | 29265. | 29647. | 30039. | 30436. | 30838 |
| 9th year. | 31899. | 32839. | 32892. | 33404. | 33922 |
| 10th year. | 34770. | 35385. | 36017. | 36661. | 37314 |
| 11th year. | 37899. | 38658. | 39439. | 40235. | 41045 |
| 12th year. | 41310. | 42234. | 43185. | 44158. | 45150 |
| 13th year. | 45028. | 46141. | 47288. | 48464. | 49665 |
| 14th year. | 49080. | 50409. | 51780. | 53189. | 54631 |
| 15th year. | 53498. | 55072. | 56699. | 58375. | 60094 |
| 16th year. | 58312. | 60166. | 62086. | 64066. | 66104 |
| 17th year. | 63561. | 65731. | 67984. | 70313. | 72714 |
| 18th year. | 69281. | 71811. | 74442. | 77168. | 79986 |
| 19th year. | 75516. | 78454. | 81514. | 84692. | 87984 |
| 20th year. | 82313. | 85711. | 89258. | 92950. | 96783 |
| Total Maturity. | 723213. | 743784. | 765108. | 787113. | 809750 |

## RD Instalmenf - 350/month

| After | 9% | 9.25% | 9.5% | 9.75% | 10% |
|---|---|---|---|---|---|
| 6th year. | 28736. | 28979. | 29230. | 29482. | 29737 |
| 7th year. | 31322. | 31659. | 32007. | 32357. | 32711 |
| 8th year. | 34141. | 34588. | 35047. | 35511. | 35982 |
| 9th year. | 37214. | 37787. | 38377. | 38974. | 39580 |
| 10th year. | 40563. | 41282. | 42023. | 42774. | 43539 |
| 11th year. | 44213. | 45101. | 46015. | 46944. | 47892 |
| 12th year. | 48193. | 49273. | 50386. | 51521. | 52682 |
| 13th year. | 52530. | 53830. | 55173. | 56545. | 57950 |
| 14th year. | 57258. | 58810. | 60414. | 62058. | 63745 |
| 15th year. | 62411. | 64250. | 66154. | 68108. | 70119 |
| 16th year. | 68028. | 70193. | 72438. | 74749. | 77131 |
| 17th year. | 74150. | 76685. | 79320. | 82037. | 84844 |
| 18th year. | 80824. | 83779. | 86855. | 90035. | 93329 |
| 19th year. | 88098. | 91528. | 95107. | 98814. | 102662 |
| 20th year. | 96027. | 99995. | 104142. | 108448. | 112928 |
| Total Maturity. | 843708. | 867739. | 892688. | 918357. | 944831 |

## RD Instalment - 400/month

| After | 9% | 9.25% | 9.5% | 9.75% | 10% |
|---|---|---|---|---|---|
| 6th year. | 32838. | 33124. | 33404. | 33697. | 33981 |
| 7th year. | 35794. | 36187. | 36577. | 36982. | 37379 |
| 8th year. | 39015. | 39535. | 40052. | 40588. | 41117 |
| 9th year. | 42527. | 43192. | 43857. | 44545. | 45229 |
| 10th year. | 46354. | 47187. | 47914. | 48888. | 49752 |
| 11th year. | 50526. | 51552. | 52466. | 53655. | 54727 |
| 12th year. | 55073. | 56320. | 57450. | 58886. | 60200 |
| 13th year. | 60030. | 61530. | 62908. | 64627. | 66220 |
| 14th year. | 65433. | 67221. | 68884. | 70929. | 72842 |
| 15th year. | 71322. | 73439. | 75428. | 77844. | 80126 |
| 16th year. | 77741. | 80233. | 82594. | 85434. | 88138 |
| 17th year. | 84737. | 87654. | 90440. | 93764. | 96952 |
| 18th year. | 92363. | 95762. | 99032. | 102906. | 106648 |
| 19th year. | 100676. | 104620. | 108440. | 112939. | 117312 |
| 20th year. | 109737. | 114297. | 118742. | 123951. | 129044 |
| Total Maturity. | 964166. | 991853. | 1018188. | 1049635. | 1079667 |

## RD Instalment 450/ month

| After | 9% | 9.25% | 9.5% | 9.75% | 10% |
|---|---|---|---|---|---|
| 6th year. | 36942. | 37265. | 37581. | 37901. | 38232 |
| 7th year. | 40267. | 40712. | 41152. | 41596. | 42055 |
| 8th year. | 43891. | 44478. | 45061. | 45652. | 46260 |
| 9th year. | 47841. | 48592. | 49342. | 50103. | 50886 |
| 10th year. | 52147. | 53087. | 54029. | 54988. | 55975 |
| 11th year. | 56840. | 57998. | 59162. | 60350. | 61572 |
| 12th year. | 61956. | 63362. | 64783. | 66234. | 67730 |
| 13th year. | 67532. | 69223. | 70937. | 72691. | 74503 |
| 14th year. | 73610. | 75627. | 77676. | 79779. | 81953 |
| 15th year. | 80235. | 82622. | 85055. | 87557. | 90148 |
| 16th year. | 87456. | 90265. | 93135. | 96094. | 99163 |
| 17th year. | 95327. | 98614. | 101983. | 105463. | 109079 |
| 18th year. | 103906. | 107736. | 111672. | 115746. | 119987 |
| 19th year. | 113258. | 110701. | 122281. | 127031. | 131986 |
| 20th year. | 123451. | 128589. | 133897. | 139417. | 145184 |
| Total Maturity. | 1084659. | 1115871. | 1147746. | 1180602. | 1214713 |

## RD Instalment 500/ month

| After | 9% | 9.25% | 9.5% | 9.75% | 10% |
|---|---|---|---|---|---|
| 6th year. | 41052. | 41404. | 41758. | 42117. | 42478 |
| 7th year. | 44746. | 45233. | 45725. | 46223. | 46725 |
| 8th year. | 48773. | 49417. | 50069. | 50730. | 51398 |
| 9th year. | 53163. | 53989. | 54825. | 55676. | 56538 |
| 10th year. | 57948. | 58983. | 60034. | 61104. | 62191 |
| 11th year. | 63163. | 64438. | 65737. | 67062. | 68411 |
| 12th year. | 68848. | 70399. | 71982. | 73600. | 75252 |
| 13th year. | 75044. | 76911. | 78820. | 80776. | 82777 |
| 14th year. | 81798. | 84025. | 86308. | 88652. | 91055 |
| 15th year. | 89160. | 91797. | 94507. | 97296. | 100160 |
| 16th year. | 97184. | 100289. | 103485. | 106782. | 110176 |
| 17th year. | 105931. | 109565. | 113317. | 117193. | 121194 |
| 18th year. | 115464. | 119700. | 124082. | 128620. | 133313 |
| 19th year. | 125856. | 130773. | 135869. | 141160. | 146644 |
| 20th year. | 137183. | 142869. | 148777. | 154923. | 161309 |
| Total maturity. | 1205313. | 1239792. | 1275295. | 1311914. | 1349621 |

# RECURRING FIXT DEPOSIT

## A. GRAPH TABLE

Table 1
1st year Open
2nd year open+1opened
3rd year open+2opened
4th year open+3opened
5th year open+4opened
6th year maturity
15th year final maturity

Table 2
1st year 1st RD for 60months(5years)
2nd year 2nd RD for 48months(4years)
3rd year 3rd RD for 36months(3years)
4th year 4th RD for 24months(2years)
5th year 5th RD for 12months(1year)
6th year maturity
15th year final maturity

## B. INVESTMENT TABLE

1st year 1×12×100=1200/-
2nd year 2×12×100=2400/-
3rd year 3×12×100=3600/-
4th year 4×12×100=4800/-
5th year 5×12×100=6000/-

Total Investmenf- 18000/-

## C. MATURITY TABLE

1st year 1st RD
1200+65
1265+1265+127=2657/-
1265+2657+266=4188/-
1265+4188+419=5872/-
1265+5872+587=7724/-
2nd year 2nd RD
1200+65
1265+1265+127=2657/-
1265+2657+266=4188/-
1265+4188+419=5872/-
3rd year 3rd RD
1200+65
1265+1265+127=2657/-
1265+2657+266=4188/-
4th year 4th RD
1200+65
1265+1265+127=2657/-
5th year 5th RD
1200+65=1265/-

After

5th year maturity 7724+5872+4188+2657+1265=21706/-
6th year 23877/-
7th year 26264/-
8th year 28891/-
9th year 31780/-
10th year 34958/-
11th year 38454/-
12th year 42299/-
13th year 46529/-
14th year 51182/-
15th year 56300/-

Final maturity- 56300/-

## D. INTEREST TABLE

Total Invest many- 18000/-

Total Interest received- 28300/-

# HOW TO DO?

## Alternative recurring deposit

You have to open 5 recurring deposit at alternate years on 1st,2nd,3rd,4th and 5th year.

At 1st year for 5years

At 2nd year for 4 years

At 3rd year for 3years

At 4th year for 2years

At 5th year for 1 year

You will receive total maturity after five year

That you invest for next 10 years or more.

After ten years you will receive final maturity.

# Few example calculation
# On
# Recurring fixt deposit

Investment Many- 18000/-
Monthly Instalment- 100/-


*****************Interest rate- 9%

After 5th year
Maturity many- 21308/-
Final Maturity after 15th year- 50445/-

*****************Interest rate- 9.25%

After 5th year
Maturity Many- 21398/-
Final maturity after 15th year- 51831/-

*****************Interest rate- 9.5%

After 5th year
Maturity many- 21505/-
Final maturity after 15th year- 53294/-

*****************Interest rate- 9.75%

After 5th year
Maturity many- 21594/-
Final maturity after 15th year- 54749/-

*****************Interest rate- 10%

After 5th year
Maturity many- 21706/-
Final maturity after 15th year- 56300/-

Investment Many- 27000/-
Monthly instalment- 150/-


\*\*\*\*\*\*\*\*\*\*\*\*\*\*\*\*\*\*Interest rate- 9%
After 5th year
Maturity many- 31956/-
Final maturity after 15th year- 75651/-

\*\*\*\*\*\*\*\*\*\*\*\*\*\*\*\*\*\*Interest rate-9.25%
After 5th year
Maturity many-32101/-
Final maturity after 15th year -77755/-

\*\*\*\*\*\*\*\*\*\*\*\*\*\*\*\*\*\*Interest rate -9.5%
After 5th year
Maturity many -32258/-
Final maturity after 15th year -79943/-

\*\*\*\*\*\*\*\*\*\*\*\*\*\*\*\*\*\*Interest rate -9.75%
After 5th year
Maturity many -32403/-
Final maturity after 15th year -82154/-

\*\*\*\*\*\*\*\*\*\*\*\*\*\*\*\*\*\*Interest rate -10%
After 5th year
Maturity many -32564/-
Final maturity after 15th year -84463/-

Investment many -36000/-
Monthly instalment -200/-

\*\*\*\*\*\*\*\*\*\*\*\*\*\*\*\*\*\*Interest rate -9%

After 5th year
Maturity many -42604/-
Final maturity many after 15th year -100859/-

\*\*\*\*\*\*\*\*\*\*\*\*\*\*\*\*\*\*Interest rate -9.25%

After 5th year
Maturity many -42798/-
Final maturity many after 15th year -103666/-

\*\*\*\*\*\*\*\*\*\*\*\*\*\*\*\*\*\*Interest rate 9.5%

After 5th year
Maturity many -43011/-
Final maturity many after 15th year -106591/-

\*\*\*\*\*\*\*\*\*\*\*\*\*\*\*\*\*\*Interest rate -9.75%

After 5th year
Maturity many -43207/-
Final maturity many after 15th year -109547/-

\*\*\*\*\*\*\*\*\*\*\*\*\*\*\*\*\*\*Interest rate -10%

After 5th year
Maturity many -43403/-
Final maturity many after 15th year -112576/-

Investment Many-45000/-
Monthly Instalment -250/-


******************Interest rate -9%

After 5th year
Maturity Many -53249/-
Final Maturity After 15th year -126060/-

******************Interest rate -9.25%

After 5th year
Maturity Many -53495/-
Final Maturity after 15th year -129577/-

******************Interest rate -9.5%

After 5th year
Maturity Many -53748/-
Final Maturity after 15th year -133200/-

******************Interest rate -9.75%

After 5th year
Maturity Many -53998/-
Final Maturity after 15th year -136906/-

******************Interest rate -10%

After 5th year
Maturity Many -54263/-
Final Maturity after 15th year -140744/-

Investment Many -54000/-
Monthly Instalment -300/-

*****************Interest rate -9%

After 5th year
Maturity Many -63912/-
Final Maturity after 15th year -151303/-

*****************Interest rate -9.25%

After 5th year
Maturity Many -64199/-
Final Maturity after 15th year -155504/-

*****************Interest rate -9.5%

After 5th year
Maturity Many -64517/-
Final Maturity after 15th year -159888/-

*****************Interest rate -9.75%

After 5th year
Maturity Many -64804
Final Maturity after 15th year -164304/-

*****************Interest rate -10%

After 5th year
Maturity Many -65109/-
Final Maturity after 15th year -168876/-

Investment Many -63000/-
Monthly Instalment -350/-


*******************Interest rate -9%

After 5th year
Maturity many -74559/-
Final maturity after 15th year -176508/-


*******************Interest rate -9.25%

After 5th year
Maturity many -74898
Final maturity after 15th year -181420/-


*******************Interest rate -9.5%

After 5th year
Maturity many -75254/-
Final maturity after 15th year -186497/-


*******************Interest rate -9.75%

After 5th year
Maturity many -75608/-
Final maturity after 15th year -191696/-


*******************Interest rate -10%

After 5th year
Maturity many -75969/-
Final maturity after 15th year -197044/-

Investment many -72000/-
Monthly instalment -400/-


*****************Interest rate 9%

After 5th year
Maturity many -85205/-
Final maturity after 15th year -201711/-

*****************Interest rate -9.25%

After 5th year
Maturity many -85611/-
Final maturity after 15th year -207369/-

*****************Interest rate -9.5%

After 5th year
Maturity many -86000/-
Final maturity after 15th year -213128/-

*****************Interest rate -9.75%

After 5th year
Maturity many -86417/-
Final maturity after 15th year -219101/-

*****************Interest rate -10%

After 5th year
Maturity many -86811/-
Final maturity after 15th year -225165/-

Investment many -81000/-
Monthly instalment -450/-


******************Interest rate -9%
After 5th year
Maturity many -95853/-
Final maturity after 15th year -226919/-

******************Interest rate -9.25%
After 5th year
Maturity many -96315
Final maturity after 15th year -233297/-

******************Interest rate -9.5%
After 5th year
Maturity many -96755/-
Final maturity many after 15th year -239781/-

******************Interest rate -9.75%
After 5th year
Maturity many -97203/-
Final maturity after 15th year -246448/-

******************Interest rate -10%
After 5th year
Maturity many -97669/-
Final maturity after 15th year -253328/-

Investment many 90000/-
Monthly Instalment 500/-


******************Interest rate 9%

After 5th year
Maturity many 106515/-
Final maturity after 15th year 252160/-


******************Interest rate 9.25%

After 5th year
Maturity many 107012/-
Final maturity after 15th year 259207/-


******************Interest rate 9.5%

After 5th year
Maturity many 107508
Final maturity after 15th year 266429


******************Interest rate 9.75%

After 5th year
Maturity many 108011/-
Final maturity after 15th year 273850/-


******************Interest rate 10%

After 5th year
Maturity many 108515/-
Final maturity after 15th year 281460/-

To,
The Readers


I will see you next time with more advantage.


Author-
Sushanta Kumar Das.

www.ingramcontent.com/pod-product-compliance
Lightning Source LLC
Chambersburg PA
CBHW071303170526
45165CB00003B/1405